ISBN 978-1-397-26142-7
PIBN 11371974

1 MONTH OF
FREE
READING

at
www.ForgottenBooks.com

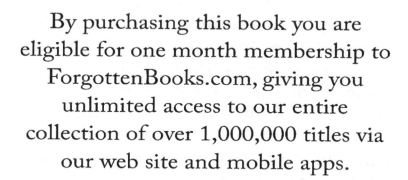

By purchasing this book you are eligible for one month membership to ForgottenBooks.com, giving you unlimited access to our entire collection of over 1,000,000 titles via our web site and mobile apps.

To claim your free month visit:
www.forgottenbooks.com/free1371974

English
Français
Deutsche
Italiano
Español
Português

www.forgottenbooks.com

Mythology Photography **Fiction**
Fishing Christianity **Art** Cooking
Essays Buddhism Freemasonry
Medicine **Biology** Music **Ancient
Egypt** Evolution Carpentry Physics
Dance Geology **Mathematics** Fitness
Shakespeare **Folklore** Yoga Marketing
Confidence Immortality Biographies
Poetry **Psychology** Witchcraft
Electronics Chemistry History **Law**
Accounting **Philosophy** Anthropology
Alchemy Drama Quantum Mechanics
Atheism Sexual Health **Ancient History**
Entrepreneurship Languages Sport
Paleontology Needlework Islam
Metaphysics Investment Archaeology
Parenting Statistics Criminology
Motivational

Historic, Archive Document

Do not assume content reflects current
scientific knowledge, policies, or practices.

U. C. DEPT. OF
NATIONAL AGRICULTURE

MAR 18 1970

CURRENT SERIAL RECORDS

WATER SUPPLY OUTLOOK FOR
COLORADO AND NEW MEXICO

and
FEDERAL - STATE - PRIVATE COOPERATIVE SNOW SURVEYS

UNITED STATES DEPARTMENT of AGRICULTURE···SOIL CONSERVATION SERVICE
and
COLORADO AGRICULTURAL EXPERIMENT STATION
STATE ENGINEER of COLORADO
and STATE ENGINEER of NEW MEXICO

Data included in this report were obtained by the agencies
named above in cooperation with the Bureau of Reclamation,
U.S. Forest Service, National Park Service, Corps of Engineers
and other Federal, State, and private organizations.

‖‖‖‖‖‖‖‖‖‖ AS OF ‖‖‖‖‖‖‖‖‖‖
MAR. 1, 1970
‖‖‖‖‖‖‖‖‖‖‖‖‖‖‖‖‖‖‖‖‖‖‖‖‖‖‖‖

TO RECIPIENTS OF WATER SUPPLY OUTLOOK REPORTS

Most of the usable water in western states originates as mountain snowfall. This snowfall accumulates during the winter and spring, several months before the snow melts and appears as streamflow. Since the runoff from precipitation as snow is delayed, estimates of snowmelt runoff can be made well in advance of its occurrence. Streamflow forecasts published in this report are based principally on measurement of the water equivalent of the mountain snowpack.

Forecasts become more accurate as more of the data affecting runoff are measured. All forecasts assume that climatic factors during the remainder of the snow accumulation and melt season will interact with a resultant average effect on runoff. Early season forecasts are therefore subject to a greater change than those made on later dates.

The snow course measurement is obtained by sampling snow depth and water equivalent at surveyed and marked locations in mountain areas. A total of about ten samples are taken at each location. The average of these are reported as snow depth and water equivalent. These measurements are repeated in the same location near the same dates each year.

Snow surveys are made monthly or semi-monthly from January 1 through June 1 in most states. There are about 1400 snow courses in Western United States and in the Columbia Basin in British Columbia. In the near future, it is anticipated that automatic snow water equivalent sensing devices along with radio telemetry will provide a continuous record of snow water equivalent at key locations.

Detailed data on snow course and soil moisture measurements are presented in state and local reports. Other data on reservoir storage, summaries of precipitation, current streamflow, and soil moisture conditions at valley elevations are also included. The report for Western United States presents a broad picture of water supply outlook conditions, including selected streamflow forecasts, summary of snow accumulation to date, and storage in larger reservoirs.

Snow survey and soil moisture data for the period of record are published by the Soil Conservation Service by states about every five years. Data for the current year is summarized in a West-wide basic data summary and published about October 1 of each year.

PUBLISHED BY SOIL CONSERVATION SERVICE

The Soil Conservation Service publishes reports following the principal snow survey dates from January 1 through June 1 in cooperation with state water administrators, agricultural experiment stations and others. Copies of the reports for Western United States and all state reports may be obtained from Soil Conservation Service, Western Regional Technical Service Center, Room 209, 701 N. W. Glisan, Portland, Oregon 97209.

Copies of state and local reports may also be obtained from state offices of the Soil Conservation Service in the following states:

STATE	ADDRESS
Alaska	P. O. Box "F", Palmer, Alaska 99645
Arizona	6029 Federal Building, Phoenix, Arizona 85025
Colorado (N. Mex.)	12417 Federal Building, Denver, Colorado 80202
Idaho	Room 345, 304 N. 8th. St., Boise, Idaho 83702
Montana	P. O. Box 98, Bozeman, Montana 59715
Nevada	P. O. Box 4850, Reno Nevada 89505
Oregon	1218 S. W. Washington St., Portland, Oregon 97205
Utah	4012 Federal Building, Salt Lake City, Utah 84111
Washington	360 U.S. Court House, Spokane, Washington 99201
Wyoming	P. O. Box 340, Casper, Wyoming 82601

PUBLISHED BY OTHER AGENCIES.

Water Supply Outlook reports prepared by other agencies include a report for California by the Water Supply Forecast and Snow Surveys Unit, California Department of Water Resources, P O Box 388, Sacramento, California 95802 --- and for British Columbia by the Department of Lands, Forests and Water Resources, Water Resources Service, Parliament Building, Victoria, British Columbia

WATER SUPPLY OUTLOOK
FOR
COLORADO AND NEW MEXICO

and
FEDERAL - STATE - PRIVATE COOPERATIVE SNOW SURVEYS

Issued by
KENNETH E. GRANT
ADMINISTRATOR
SOIL CONSERVATION SERVICE
WASHINGTON, D.C.

||||||||||||||||||||||||||||||||||||||||||||||||||||||||||||||||||||||||||||||||||||||||||||||||||||||||||||||||||||||||||||||||||||||||||||||||||||||||||||

Released by

FRED A. MARK
STATE CONSERVATIONIST
SOIL CONSERVATION SERVICE
DENVER, COLORADO

KENNETH L. WILLIAMS
STATE CONSERVATIONIST
SOIL CONSERVATION SERVICE
ALBUQUERQUE, NEW MEXICO

In Cooperation with

RUE JENSEN
DIRECTOR
COLORADO AGRICULTURAL
EXPERIMENT STATION

S. E. REYNOLDS
STATE ENGINEER
STATE OF NEW MEXICO

C. J. KUIPER
STATE ENGINEER
STATE OF COLORADO

||||||||||||||||||||||||||||||||||||||||||||||||||||||||||||||||||||||||||||||||||||||||||||||||||||||||||||||||||||||||||||||||||||||||||||||||||||||||||||

Report prepared by

JACK N. WASHICHEK, Snow Survey Supervisor
and
RONALD E. MORELAND, Assistant Snow Survey Supervisor
SOIL CONSERVATION SERVICE
SPRUCE HALL
COLORADO STATE UNIVERSITY
FT. COLLINS, COLORADO 80521

TABLE OF CONTENTS

WATER SUPPLY OUTLOOK BY MAJOR WATERSHED AREAS

WATER SUPPLY OUTLOOK

as of
March 1, 1970

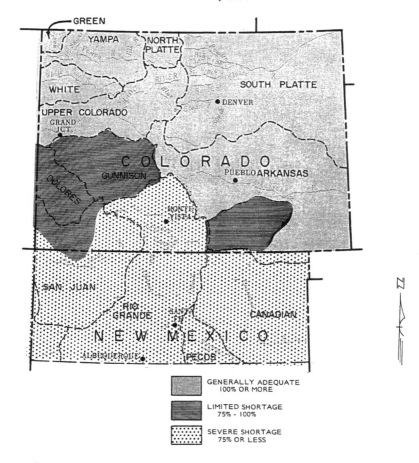

GENERALLY ADEQUATE
100% OR MORE

LIMITED SHORTAGE
75% - 100%

SEVERE SHORTAGE
75% OR LESS

The map on this page indicates the most probable water supply as of the date of this report. Estimates assume average conditions of snow fall, precipitation and other factors from this date to the end of the forecast period. As the season progresses accuracy of estimates improve. In addition to expected streamflow, reservoir storage, soil moisture in irrigated areas, and other factors are considered in estimating water supply. Estimates apply to irrigated areas along the main streams and may not indicate conditions on small tributaries.

- GENERAL SERIES PAPER NO. 901
COLORADO AGRICULTURAL EXPERIMENT STATION

WATER SUPPLY CONDITIONS
as of
March 1, 1970

THE SNOW PACK IN NORTHERN COLORADO REMAINS EXCELLENT. THE MIDDLE AREA OF COLORADO HAS ABOUT AVERAGE SNOW AND THE SNOW IN LOWER PORTION OF COLORADO AND NORTHERN NEW MEXICO IS VERY DEFICIENT.

WATER SHORTAGES WILL EXIST IN SOUTHERN COLORADO AND NEW MEXICO UNLESS THE NEXT TWO MONTHS PRODUCES MUCH ABOVE NORMAL SNOW.

FEBRUARY WAS ONE OF THE WARMEST AND DRIEST ON RECORD. RADIATION HAS EATEN AWAY MUCH OF THE SNOW ON SOUTH FACING SLOPES. LOW ELEVATION SNOWS HAVE DISAPPEARED.

CARRY-OVER RESERVOIR STORAGE IS EXCELLENT IN BOTH STATES AND WILL PROVIDE GOOD SUPPLEMENT TO EXPECTED STREAMFLOWS. ALL AREAS OF BOTH STATES EXCEPT THE LOWER RIO GRANDE ARE REPORTING GOOD SOIL MOISTURE IN THE IRRIGATED AREAS.

COLORADO-- THE SNOW PACK DECLINED OVER THE ENTIRE STATE. THE SNOW FALL WAS LESS THAN NORMAL AND TEMPERATURES WERE MUCH ABOVE NORMAL. LOW ELEVATION SNOWS HAVE BEEN EVAPORATED OR MELTED AWAY. SOUTHERN EXPOSED SLOPES HAVE BEEN SUBJECT TO INTENSE RADIATION ALL MONTH. THE MIDDLE AND NORTHERN PARTS OF THE STATE SHOULD STILL HAVE ADEQUATE WATER SUPPLIES, WHILE THE SOUTHERN PORTION WILL EXPERIENCE SHORT SUPPLIES. DESPITE THE WARM, DRY, WEATHER, MOST AREAS OF THE STATE ARE REPORTING GOOD SOIL MOISTURE. SOME REPORTS INDICATE THE SURFACE LAYERS OF SOIL AS DRY, BUT GOOD MOISTURE DOWN A FEW INCHES. RESERVOIR STORAGE IS GOOD AND WILL PROVIDE AN EXCELLENT SUPPLEMENT. MORE SNOW IS NEEDED TO INSURE ADEQUATE SUPPLIES IN SOUTHERN HALF OF THE STATE.

NEW MEXICO-- THE SNOWFALL MUST BE MUCH ABOVE NORMAL DURING MARCH OR VERY SHORT WATER SUPPLIES CAN BE EXPECTED IN ALL AREAS OF NEW MEXICO SUPPLIED BY SNOW MELT WATER. THE CURRENT SNOW PACK IS APPROACHING THE MINIMUM OF RECORD. MANY SNOW COURSES SHOW LESS SNOW ON MARCH FIRST THAN FEBRUARY FIRST. SNOWFALL DURING THE MONTH WAS DEFICIENT AND RADIATION ATE AWAY AT THE SOUTH EXPOSED SLOPES. MANY OF THE SOUTHERN SLOPES ARE BARE. RESERVOIR STORAGE IS UP FROM LAST YEAR AND WILL PROVIDE SOME SUPPLEMENT TO STREAMFLOW. SOIL MOISTURE IN THE MIDDLE AND SOUTHERN PORTIONS OF THE STATE IS REPORTED AS FAIR. THE NORTHERN PORTION HAS GOOD SOIL MOISTURE.

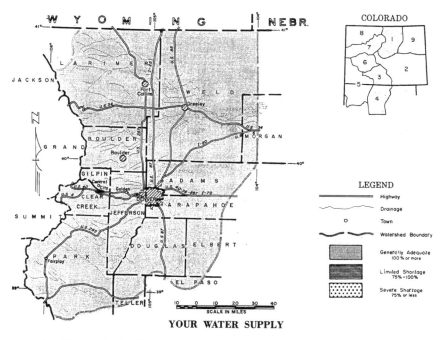

YOUR WATER SUPPLY

THE SNOW PACK ON THE SOUTH PLATTE DRAINAGE CONTINUES TO BE MUCH ABOVE AVERAGE. STREAMFLOW FORECASTS RANGE FROM 116% ON THE CACHE LA POUDRE TO 136% ON THE ST. VRAIN. SUMMER WATER SUPPLIES SHOULD BE ADEQUATE. RESERVOIR STORAGE IS GOOD WITH 112% OF LAST YEARS AND 133% OF THE 1953-67 AVERAGE.

SOIL MOISTURE CONDITIONS IN THE IRRIGATED AREAS ARE REPORTED TO BE GOOD. FEBRUARY'S WARM TEMPERATURES HAS DRIED OUT THE SURFACE SOILS.

This report prepared by
JACK N. WASHICHEK and RONALD E. MORELAND
SOIL CONSERVATION SERVICE, COLORADO STATE UNIVERSITY
FORT COLLINS, COLORADO

Issued by
F A MARK—STATE CONSERVATIONIST   E A NICHOLSON--AREA CONSERVATIONIST
U. S. DEPARTMENT OF AGRICULTURE - SOIL CONSERVATION SERVICE
DENVER COLORADO   DENVER COLORADO

The Conservation of Water begins with the Snow Survey

STREAMFLOW FORECASTS (1000 Ac. Ft.) Apr-Sept

FORECAST POINT and Forecast Period	Forecast	*	Average+
Big Thompson at			
Drake (2)	125	125	100
Boulder at Orodell	60	122	49
Cache La Poudre at			
Canon Mouth (1)	250	116	215
Clear Cr. at Golden	160	134	119
Saint Vrain at Lyons	95	136	70

(1) Observed flow minus by-pass to power plants.
(2) Observed flow minus trans-basin diversions plus municipal and irrigation diversions.
(3) Observed flow minus diversion through August P. Gumlick Tunnel.
(4) Observed flow minus change in storage in Price Reservoir.

WATER SUPPLY OUTLOOK
Expressed as "Poor, Fair, Average, Excellent" With Respect to Usual Supply.

STREAM or AREA	Flow Period	
	Spring Season	Late Season
Bear Creek	Exc.	Avg.
Coal Creek	Exc.	Avg.
North Fork of South		
Platte	Exc.	Avg.
North Fork of Cache		
La Poudre	Exc.	Avg.
Ralston Creek	Exc.	Avg.
Rock Creek	Exc.	Avg.

SUMMARY of SNOW MEASUREMENTS
(COMPARISON WITH PREVIOUS YEARS)

RIVER BASIN and/or SUB-WATERSHED	Number of Courses Averaged	THIS YEAR'S SNOW WATER AS PERCENT OF	
		Last Year	Average +
Big Thompson	5	156	146
Boulder	3	192	140
Cache La Poudre	8	133	145
Clear Creek	6	174	146
Saint Vrain	2	179	149
South Platte	3	163	147

SOIL MOISTURE

RIVER BASIN	Number of Stations	THIS YEAR'S MOISTURE as PERCENT OF:	
		Last Year	Average +
Big Thompson	3	136	124
Boulder	1	87	92
Cache La Poudre	2	173	148
Clear Creek	2	128	110
Saint Vrain	2	119	119
South Platte	2	107	100

RESERVOIR STORAGE (Thousand Ac. Ft.) END OF MONTH

RESERVOIR	Usable Capacity	Usable Storage		
		This Year	Last Year	Average +
Antero	33.0	15.9	15.9	10.6
Barr Lake	32.2	24.9	24.7	18.9
Black Hollow	8.0	4.0	3.7	3.3
Boyd Lake	44.0	30.4	38.4	27.8
Cache La Poudre	9.5	8.4	4.7	7.0
Carter Lake	108.9	91.3	90.3	71.3
Chambers Lake	8.8	3.0	2.6	2.7
Cheesman	79.0	79.1	40.6	46.4
Cobb Lake	34.0	18.5	14.6	9.9
Eleven Mile	97.8	96.4	94.6	72.0
Fossil Creek	11.6	9.9	6.2	6.1
Gross	43.1	37.4	35.1	24.0

RESERVOIR STORAGE (Thousand Ac. Ft.) END OF MONTH

RESERVOIR	Usable Capacity	Usable Storage		
		This Year	Last Year	Average +
Halligan	6.4	5.9	4.5	3.8
Horsetooth	143.5	93.3	98.4	93.6
Lake Loveland	14.3	12.0	4.2	8.1
Lone Tree	9.2	8.1	1.6	6.2
Mariano	5.4	5.1	5.5	3.9
Marshall	10.3	5.4	2.1	2.5
Marston	18.0	16.0	13.8	14.3
Milton	24.4	13.4	14.6	9.5
Standley	42.0	23.0	24.9	9.8
Terry Lake	8.2	0.0	4.4	4.9
Union	12.7	11.3	3.7	7.5
Windsor	18.6	13.0	10.9	8.4

*1933-1967 period.

*This year in percent of

CO-1b

WATER SUPPLY OUTLOOK
FOR THE SOIL CONSERVATION DISTRICTS IN THE
ARKANSAS RIVER WATERSHED IN COLORADO
as of
March 1, 1970

U. S. DEPARTMENT OF AGRICULTURE · SOIL CONSERVATION SERVICE
COLORADO EXPERIMENT STATION, STATE ENGINEERS OF COLORADO AND NEW MEXICO

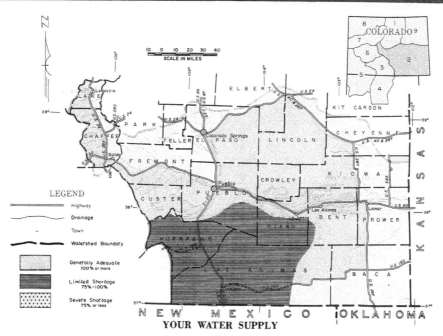

YOUR WATER SUPPLY

THE SNOW PACK IN UPPER ARKANSAS IS 124% OF THE 1953-67 AVERAGE. MOST OF
THE ABOVE AVERAGE SNOW PACK IS IN THE LEADVILLE AREA. THE CUCHARAS AND
PURGATORIE SNOW PACK IS 71%. THIS IS LESS THAN LAST MONTH DUE TO BELOW NORMAL
SNOWFALL AND WARM TEMPERATURES. THE RESERVOIR STORAGE IS GOOD WITH 376% OF LAST
YEAR'S AND 170% OF AVERAGE. SOIL MOISTURE CONDITIONS IN THE IRRIGATED AREAS IS
FAIR TO GOOD. STREAMFLOW FORECASTS ON THE ARKANSAS AND ITS TRIBUTARIES ARE
SLIGHTLY BELOW AVERAGE. MORE SNOW IS NEEDED TO ASSURE ADEQUATE WATER FOR SUMMER.

This report prepared by
JACK N. WASHICHEK and RONALD E. MORELAND
SOIL CONSERVATION SERVICE, COLORADO STATE UNIVERSITY
FORT COLLINS, COLORADO

Issued by
F. A. MARK—STATE CONSERVATIONIST   W. D. McCORKLE—AREA CONSERVATIONIST
U. S. DEPARTMENT OF AGRICULTURE - SOIL CONSERVATION SERVICE
DENVER, COLORADO   LA JUNTA, COLORADO

The Conservation of Water begins with the Snow Survey

STREAMFLOW FORECASTS (1000 Ac. Ft.) Apr-Sept

FORECAST POINT and Forecast Period	Forecast	*	Average +
Arkansas nr Pueblo (1)	270	91	298
Ark. at Salida (1)	290	94	309
Cucharas nr LaVeta	14	117	12
Purgatoire at Trinidad	40	87	46

(1) Observed flow plus change in Clear Creek, Twin Lakes, and Turquoise Reservoirs minus diversions through Busk-Ivanhoe, Divide, Twin Lakes and Homestake Tunnels and Ewing, Front Pass, Wurtz and Colombine ditches.

WATER SUPPLY OUTLOOK

Expressed as "Poor, Fair, Average, Excellent" With Respect to Usual Supply.

STREAM or AREA	Flow Period	
	Spring Season	Late Season
Apishapa	Avg.	Avg.
Fountain Creek	Avg.	Avg.
Grape	Avg.	Avg.
Hardscrable Creek	Avg.	Avg.
Huerfano	Avg.	Avg.
Monument Creek	Avg.	Avg.

SUMMARY of SNOW MEASUREMENTS
(COMPARISON WITH PREVIOUS YEARS)

RIVER BASIN and/or SUB-WATERSHED	Number of Courses Averaged	THIS YEAR'S SNOW WATER AS PERCENT OF	
		Last Year	Average +
Arkansas	10	128	124
Cucharas and Purgatoire	2	85	71

SOIL MOISTURE

RIVER BASIN	Number of Stations	THIS YEAR'S MOISTURE as PERCENT OF:	
		Last Year	Average +
Arkansas	3	135	104
Cucharas and Purgatoire	1	82	114

RESERVOIR STORAGE (Thousand Ac. Ft.) END OF MONTH

RESERVOIR	Usable Capacity	Usable Storage		
		This Year	Last Year	Average +
Adobe	61.6	18.4	0.0	11.5
Clear Creek	11.4	10.2	8.0	6.6
Cucharas	40.0	1.5	0.7	6.9
Great Plains	150.0	118.4	6.7	35.4
Horse Creek	26.9	20.9	0.4	4.9

RESERVOIR STORAGE (Thousand Ac. Ft.) END OF MONTH

RESERVOIR	Usable Capacity	Usable Storage		
		This Year	Last Year	Average +
John Martin	353.9	46.8	15.8	85.1
Meredith	41.9	25.4	0.0	9.0
Model	15.0	1.4	1.5	3.1
Turquoise	130.0	42.8	26.6	7.0
Twin Lakes	57.9	36.6	26.0	20.1

+ 1953-1967 period.

*This year in percent of avg.

Return if not delivered
UNITED STATES DEPARTMENT OF AGRICULTURE
SOIL CONSERVATION SERVICE
SNOW SURVEY
COLORADO STATE UNIVERSITY
FORT COLLINS, COLORADO 80521

OFFICIAL BUSINESS

POSTAGE AND FEES PAID
U S DEPARTMENT OF AGRICULTURE

FIRST CLASS MAIL

CO-2b

WATER SUPPLY OUTLOOK
FOR THE SOIL CONSERVATION DISTRICTS IN THE
UPPER RIO GRANDE WATERSHED IN COLORADO
as of
March 1, 1970

U.S. DEPARTMENT OF AGRICULTURE · SOIL CONSERVATION SERVICE
COLORADO EXPERIMENT STATION, STATE ENGINEERS OF COLORADO AND NEW MEXICO

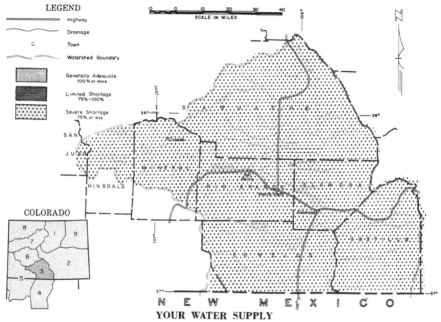

YOUR WATER SUPPLY

THE SNOW PACK IN THIS AREA IS VERY DEFICIENT. SOME SNOW COURSES ARE APPROACHING THE MINIMUM OF RECORD. UNLESS THE NEXT COUPLE OF MONTHS PRODUCE MUCH ABOVE NORMAL SNOW, WATER SHORTAGES WILL EXIST THIS SUMMER.

MOUNTAIN SOILS CONTAIN GOOD MOISTURE AND WILL TEND TO INCREASE RUNOFF. RESERVOIR STORAGE IS 169% OF AVERAGE AND WILL PROVIDE SOME SUPPLEMENT TO EXPECTED STREAMFLOW.

This report prepared by
JACK N. WASHICHEK and RONALD E. MORELAND
SOIL CONSERVATION SERVICE · COLORADO STATE UNIVERSITY
FORT COLLINS, COLORADO

Issued by
F A MARK—STATE CONSERVATIONIST   DONALD B. TOOTELL—AREA CONSERVATIONIST
U. S. DEPARTMENT OF AGRICULTURE - SOIL CONSERVATION SERVICE
DENVER COLORADO   DURANGO, COLORADO

The Conservation of Water begins with the Snow Survey

STREAMFLOW FORECASTS (1000 Ac. Ft.) Apr–Sept

FORECAST POINT and Forecast Period	Forecast	*	Average [+]
Alamosa abv Terrace	40	65	62
Conejos nr Mogote(1)	115	63	182
Culebra at San Luis (2)	15	79	19
Rio Gr. at 30 Mile Bridge (3)	90	77	117
Rio Gr. nr Del Norte (3)	320	73	438
So. Fk. at So. Fk	75	68	110

(1) Observed flow plus change in storage in Platoro Reservoir.
(2) Observed flow plus change in storage in Sanchez Reservoir.
(3) Observed flow plus change in storage in Santa Maria, Rio Grande and Continental Reservoirs.

WATER SUPPLY OUTLOOK
Expressed as "Poor, Fair, Average, Excellent" With Respect to Usual Supply.

STREAM or AREA	Spring Season	Late Season
	Flow Period	
Saguache Creek	Poor	Poor
Sangre de Cristo Cr.	Poor	Poor
Trinchera Creek	Poor	Poor

SUMMARY of SNOW MEASUREMENTS
(COMPARISON WITH PREVIOUS YEARS)

RIVER BASIN and/or SUB-WATERSHED	Number of Courses Averaged	THIS YEAR'S SNOW WATER AS PERCENT OF Last Year	Average [+]
Alamosa	2	41	49
Conejos	3	37	48
Culebra	2	71	70
Rio Grande	10	54	66

SOIL MOISTURE

RIVER BASIN	Number of Stations	THIS YEAR'S MOISTURE as PERCENT OF: Last Year	Average [+]
Alamosa	2	150	131
Conejos	1	151	129
Culebra	1	86	109
Rio Grande	3	112	124

RESERVOIR STORAGE (Thousand Ac. Ft.) END OF MONTH

RESERVOIR	Usable Capacity	This Year	Last Year	Average [+]
Continental	26.7	6.2	6.4	4.4
Platoro	60.0	3.0	3.0	7.1
Rio Grande	45.8	27.7	21.3	12.0

RESERVOIR STORAGE (Thousand Ac. Ft.) END OF MONTH

RESERVOIR	Usable Capacity	This Year	Last Year	Average [+]
Sanchez	103.2	19.0	11.8	10.6
Santa Maria	45.0	6.3	3.8	5.5
Terrace	17.7	11.0	11.2	3.7

+ 1953-1967 period.

Return if not delivered
UNITED STATES DEPARTMENT OF AGRICULTURE
SOIL CONSERVATION SERVICE
SNOW SURVEY
COLORADO STATE UNIVERSITY
FORT COLLINS, COLORADO 80521

OFFICIAL BUSINESS

*This year in percent of avg.

CO-3b

WATER SUPPLY OUTLOOK
FOR THE SOIL CONSERVATION DISTRICTS IN THE
RIO GRANDE WATERSHED IN NEW MEXICO

as of

March 1, 1970

U. S. DEPARTMENT OF AGRICULTURE · SOIL CONSERVATION SERVICE
COLORADO EXPERIMENT STATION, STATE ENGINEERS OF COLORADO AND NEW MEXICO

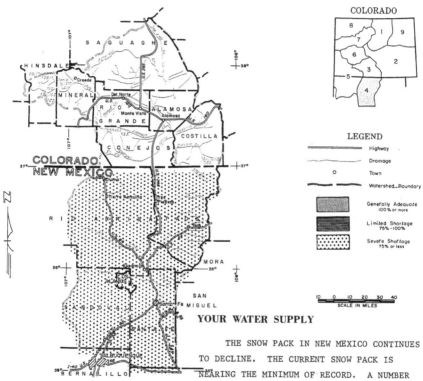

COLORADO

LEGEND

	Highway
	Drainage
O	Town
	Watershed Boundary
	Generally Adequate 100% or more
	Limited Shortage 75%-100%
	Severe Shortage 75% or less

SCALE IN MILES
10   0   10   20   30   40

YOUR WATER SUPPLY

THE SNOW PACK IN NEW MEXICO CONTINUES TO DECLINE. THE CURRENT SNOW PACK IS NEARING THE MINIMUM OF RECORD. A NUMBER OF SNOW COURSES ARE ALREADY AT A MINIMUM. WATER SHORTAGES WILL EXIST ALL OVER THE STATE UNLESS SNOWFALL DURING MARCH IS MUCH ABOVE NORMAL.

RESERVOIR STORAGE IS GOOD AND WILL BE AN EXCELLENT SUPPLEMENT THIS SUMMER.

This report prepared by
JACK N. WASHICHEK and RONALD E. MORELAND
SOIL CONSERVATION SERVICE, COLORADO STATE UNIVERSITY
FORT COLLINS, COLORADO

Issued by
KENNETH L. WILLIAMS—STATE CONSERVATIONIST   RICHARD S SWENSON—AREA CONSERVATIONIST
U. S. DEPARTMENT OF AGRICULTURE - SOIL CONSERVATION SERVICE
ALBUQUERQUE, NEW MEXICO   SANTA FE, NEW MEXICO

The Conservation of Water begins with the Snow Survey

STREAMFLOW FORECASTS (1000 Ac. Ft.) Mar–Jul

FORECAST POINT and Forecast Period	Forecast		Average +
Costilla at Cost.(1)	10	56	18
Pecos at Pecos	24	59	41
Rio Chama to ElVado	120	64	188
Rio Gr. at Otowi (2)	300	58	513
Rio Gr. at San Mar(2)	160	48	334
Rio Hondo nr Valdez	10	67	15
Red R. at mouth nr Questa	23	72	32

The forecast of the Rio Grande at San Marcial is 25% of the Average used by the Elephant Butte Irrigation District.
(1) Observed flow plus change in Costilla Reservoir.
(2) Observed flow plus change in storage in El Vado and Abiquiu Reservoir.

WATER SUPPLY OUTLOOK

Expressed as "Poor, Fair, Average, Excellent" With Respect to Usual Supply.

STREAM or AREA	Flow Period	
	Spring Season	Late Season
Embudo Creek	Poor	Poor
Jemez River	Poor	Poor
Mora River	Poor	Poor
Nambe Creek	Poor	Poor
Rio Ojo Caliante	Poor	Poor
Rio Pueblo de Taos	Poor	Poor
Santa Fe Creek	Poor	Poor

SUMMARY of SNOW MEASUREMENTS
(COMPARISON WITH PREVIOUS YEARS)

RIVER BASIN and/or SUB-WATERSHED	Number of Courses Averaged	THIS YEAR'S SNOW WATER AS PERCENT OF	
		Last Year	Average +
Pecos	1	6	6
Rio Chama	4	30	48
Rio Grande, N.M.	12	39	45
Rio Hondo	1	62	--
Red River	2	54	55

SOIL MOISTURE

RIVER BASIN	Number of Stations	THIS YEAR'S MOISTURE as PERCENT OF:	
		Last Year	Average +
Pecos	2	53	75
Rio Chama	2	84	73
Rio Grande	4	68	80
Red River	1	94	79

RESERVOIR STORAGE (Thousand Ac. Ft.) END OF MONTH

RESERVOIR	Usable Capacity	Usable Storage		
		This Year	Last Year	Average +
Alamorgordo	111	80	68	76
Caballo	344	81	60	81
Conchas	273	232	124	163
Elephant Butte	2195	574	406	370

RESERVOIR STORAGE (Thousand Ac. Ft.) END OF MONTH

RESERVOIR	Usable Capacity	Usable Storage		
		This Year	Last Year	Average +
ElVado	195	1	1	4
McMillen-Avalon	32	38	8	20

+ 1953–1967 period.

*This year in percent of avg.

FIRST CLASS MAIL

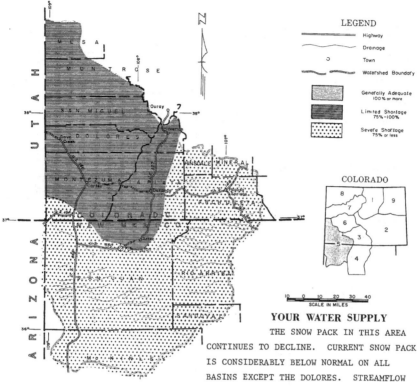

LEGEND

——————— Highway
~~~~~~~ Drainage
○ Town
⌐⌐⌐⌐⌐ Watershed Boundary

Generally Adequate
100 % or more

Limited Shortage
75%-100%

Severe Shortage
75% or less

COLORADO

SCALE IN MILES
10 0 10 20 30 40

YOUR WATER SUPPLY

THE SNOW PACK IN THIS AREA CONTINUES TO DECLINE. CURRENT SNOW PACK IS CONSIDERABLY BELOW NORMAL ON ALL BASINS EXCEPT THE DOLORES. STREAMFLOW FORECASTS FOLLOW A SIMILAR PATTERN. ALL STREAMS WILL FLOW MUCH BELOW NORMAL UNLESS THE NEXT TWO MONTHS PRODUCE MUCH ABOVE AVERAGE SNOW.

CARRY-OVER STORAGE IN THE BASIN'S RESERVOIR IS GOOD. SOIL MOISTURE IS REPORTED AS GOOD.

This report prepared by
JACK N. WASHICHEK and RONALD E. MORELAND
SOIL CONSERVATION SERVICE, COLORADO STATE UNIVERSITY
FORT COLLINS, COLORADO

Issued by
F. A. MARK—STATE CONSERVATIONIST   KENNETH L. WILLIAMS—STATE CONSERVATIONIST
DENVER, COLORADO   ALBUQUERQUE, NEW MEXICO
U S   DEPARTMENT OF AGRICULTURE - SOIL CONSERVATION SERVICE
DONALD R. TOOTELL—AREA CONSERVATIONIST   RICHARD S. SWENSON I—AREA CONSERVATIONIST
DURANGO, COLORADO   SANTA FE, NEW MEXICO

The Conservation of Water begins with the Snow Survey

STREAMFLOW FORECASTS (1000 Ac. Ft.) Apr-Sept

FORECAST POINT and Forecast Period	Forecast	*	Average +
Animas at Durango	320	78	409
Dolores at Dolores	180	78	231
La Plata at Hesperus	15	63	24
Los Pinos at Bayfield (1)	125	64	194
Piedra Cr. at Piedra	90	55	163
San Juan at Carracas	250	66	379
Inflow to Navajo Res (1)(Apr-Jul)	420	68	619

(1) Observed flow plus change in storage in Vallecito Reservoir

WATER SUPPLY OUTLOOK
Expressed as "Poor, Fair, Average, Excellent" With Respect to Usual Supply.

STREAM or AREA	Flow Period	
	Spring Season	Late Season
Florida	Fair	Poor
Mancos	Fair	Poor
San Miguel	Fair	Poor

SUMMARY of SNOW MEASUREMENTS
(COMPARISON WITH PREVIOUS YEARS)

RIVER BASIN and/or SUB-WATERSHED	Number of Courses Averaged	THIS YEAR'S SNOW WATER AS PERCENT OF	
		Last Year	Average +
Animas	6	51	76
Dolores	4	59	98
San Juan	5	42	57

SOIL MOISTURE

RIVER BASIN	Number of Stations	THIS YEAR'S MOISTURE as PERCENT OF:	
		Last Year	Average +
Animas	3	155	89
Dolores	3	121	92
San Juan	2	143	104

RESERVOIR STORAGE (Thousand Ac. Ft.) END OF MONTH

RESERVOIR	Usable Capacity	Usable Storage		
		This Year	Last Year	Average +
Groundhog	22	13	13	7
Lemon	40	30	22	15
Navajo	1036	926	870	
Vallecito	126	75	69	48

RESERVOIR STORAGE (Thousand Ac. Ft.) END OF MONTH

RESERVOIR	Usable Capacity	Usable Storage		
		This Year	Last Year	Average +

+ 1953-1967 period.

*This year in percent of avg.

Return if not delivered
UNITED STATES DEPARTMENT OF AGRICULTURE
SOIL CONSERVATION SERVICE
SNOW SURVEY
COLORADO STATE UNIVERSITY
FORT COLLINS, COLORADO 80521

OFFICIAL BUSINESS

POSTAGE AND FEES PAID
U S DEPARTMENT OF AGRICULTURE

FIRST CLASS MAIL

WATER SUPPLY OUTLOOK
FOR THE SOIL CONSERVATION DISTRICTS IN THE
GUNNISON RIVER WATERSHED IN COLORADO
as of

March 1, 1970

U.S. DEPARTMENT OF AGRICULTURE · SOIL CONSERVATION SERVICE
COLORADO EXPERIMENT STATION, STATE ENGINEERS OF COLORADO AND NEW MEXICO

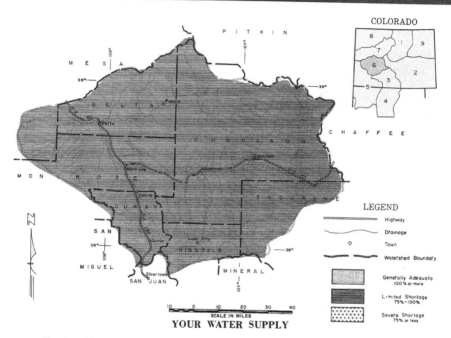

LEGEND

————————	Highway
∿∿∿∿∿∿	Drainage
○	Town
▬▬▬▬▬	Watershed Boundary
	Generally Adequate 100% or more
	Limited Shortage 75%-100%
	Severe Shortage 75% or less

SCALE IN MILES

YOUR WATER SUPPLY

FOR THE FIRST TIME THIS YEAR THE SNOW PACK IN THIS AREA HAS FALLEN BELOW NORMAL. ONLY SCATTERED SNOW FELL DURING THE MONTH AND WARM TEMPERATURES WERE THE RULE.

STREAMFLOW FORECASTS RANGE FROM 85% OF THE 15 YEAR NORMAL ON THE UNCOMPAHGRE TO 94% ON SURFACE CREEK.

THIS SHOULD STILL PROVIDE NEAR ADEQUATE WATER SUPPLIES.

CARRY-OVER STORAGE IS GOOD. SOIL MOISTURE CONDITIONS ARE REPORTED AS GOOD.

This report prepared by
JACK N. WASHICHEK and RONALD E. MORELAND
SOIL CONSERVATION SERVICE, COLORADO STATE UNIVERSITY
FORT COLLINS, COLORADO

Issued by
F. A. MARK—STATE CONSERVATIONIST   DEARL BEACH—AREA CONSERVATIONIST
U. S. DEPARTMENT OF AGRICULTURE – SOIL CONSERVATION SERVICE
DENVER, COLORADO   GRAND JUNCTION, COLORADO

The Conservation of Water begins with the Snow Survey

STREAMFLOW FORECASTS (1000 Ac. Ft.) Apr–Sept

FORECAST POINT and Forecast Period	Forecast		Average +
Gunnison nr Gr. Junction	1000	* 87	1137
Surface Cr. nr Cedaridge	15	94	16
Uncomphagre at Colona	110	85	129

(1) Observed flow plus change in storage in Blue Mesa and Morrow Point Reservoirs.

WATER SUPPLY OUTLOOK
Expressed as "Poor, Fair, Average, Excellent" With Respect to Usual Supply.

STREAM or AREA	Flow Period	
	Spring Season	Late Season
North Fork of Gunnison	Avg.	Avg.
Taylor	Avg.	Avg.

SUMMARY of SNOW MEASUREMENTS
(COMPARISON WITH PREVIOUS YEARS)

RIVER BASIN and/or SUB-WATERSHED	Number of Courses Averaged	THIS YEAR'S SNOW WATER AS PERCENT OF	
		Last Year	Average +
Gunnison	12	81	107
Surface Creek	3	59	90
Uncompahgre	3	85	114

SOIL MOISTURE

RIVER BASIN	Number of Stations	THIS YEAR'S MOISTURE as PERCENT OF:	
		Last Year	Average +
Gunnison	1	105	116
Surface Creek	1	109	100
Uncompahgre	1	109	100

RESERVOIR STORAGE (Thousand Ac. Ft.) END OF MONTH

RESERVOIR	Usable Capacity	Usable Storage		
		This Year	Last Year	Average +
Blue Mesa	941	500	422	--
Morrow Point	121	85	49	--
Taylor	106	97	39	56

RESERVOIR STORAGE (Thousand Ac. Ft.) END OF MONTH

RESERVOIR	Usable Capacity	Usable Storage		
		This Year	Last Year	Average +

+ 1953–1967 period.

*This year in percent of avg.

Return if not delivered
UNITED STATES DEPARTMENT OF AGRICULTURE
SOIL CONSERVATION SERVICE
SNOW SURVEY
COLORADO STATE UNIVERSITY
FORT COLLINS, COLORADO 80521

OFFICIAL BUSINESS

POSTAGE AND FEES PAID
U S DEPARTMENT OF AGRICULTURE

FIRST CLASS MAIL

CO-6b

WATER SUPPLY OUTLOOK
FOR THE SOIL CONSERVATION DISTRICTS IN THE
COLORADO RIVER WATERSHED IN COLORADO
as of

March 1, 1970

U. S. DEPARTMENT OF AGRICULTURE · SOIL CONSERVATION SERVICE
COLORADO EXPERIMENT STATION, STATE ENGINEERS OF COLORADO AND NEW MEXICO

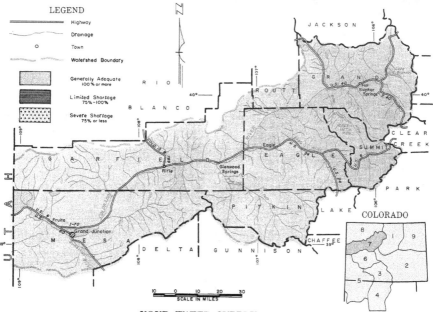

YOUR WATER SUPPLY

SNOW PACK IN THE UPPER COLORADO BASIN DID NOT GAIN MUCH DURING FEBRUARY. THE ABOVE SEASONAL TEMPERATURES TOOK ITS TOLL OF THE SNOW, ESPECIALLY AT THE LOW ELEVATIONS AND SOUTH EXPOSED SLOPES.

FORECASTS STILL REMAIN GOOD AND NEAR NORMAL WATER SUPPLIES ARE STILL EXPECTED.

SOIL MOISTURE CONDITIONS IN THE IRRIGATED AREAS IS REPORTED AS GOOD. RESERVOIR STORAGE IS ABOVE NORMAL.

This report prepared by

JACK N. WASHICHEK and RONALD E. MORELAND
SOIL CONSERVATION SERVICE- COLORADO STATE UNIVERSITY
FORT COLLINS, COLORADO

Issued by

F. A. MARK
STATE CONSERVATIONIST
DENVER, COLORADO

R.L. PORTER
AREA CONSERVATIONIST
GLENWOOD SPRINGS, COLORADO

D B BEACH
AREA CONSERVATIONIST
GRAND JUNCTION, COLORADO

U S DEPARTMENT OF AGRICULTURE - SOIL CONSERVATION SERVICE

The Conservation of Water begins with the Snow Survey

STREAMFLOW FORECASTS (1000 Ac. Ft.) Apr-Sept

FORECAST POINT and Forecast Period	Forecast	*	Average †
Blue ab Gr. Mt. (1)	300	127	236
Colo Rv inflow to			
Granby Res. (2)	225	103	219
Colo Rv nr Dotsero(3)	1400	102	1375
Roar. Fk at GlSpr.(4)	650	93	692
Wm. Fk nr Par. (5)	80	133	60
Will. Cr. inflow to			
Will. Cr. Res.	58	126	46
Colo. nr Cameo (6)	2250	102	2216

WATER SUPPLY OUTLOOK
Expressed as "Poor, Fair, Average, Excellent" With Respect to Usual Supply.

STREAM or AREA	Flow Period	
	Spring Season	Late Season
Brush	Exc.	Avg.
Eagle River	Exc.	Avg.
Gypsum Creek	Exc.	Avg.

(1) Observed flow plus diversions through Roberts Tunnel and change in storage in Dillon Reservoir.
(2) Observed flow corrected for change in storage in Lake Granby as furnished by U.S.B.R. and diversions by Adams Tunnel and Grand River Ditch.
(3) Observed flow plus the changes as indicated in (1), (2) and (5) plus Moffat Ditch and change in Homestake, Williams Fork, Green Mt. and Willow Creek Reservoirs.
(4) Observed flow plus diversions through Divide and Twin Lakes Tunnels plus change in storage in Ruedi Reservoir.
(5) Observed flow plus diversions through August P. Gumlick Tunnel.
(6) Observed flow plus the changes as indicated in (3) and (4).

SUMMARY of SNOW MEASUREMENTS
(COMPARISON WITH PREVIOUS YEARS)

RIVER BASIN and/or SUB-WATERSHED	Number of Courses Averaged	THIS YEAR'S SNOW WATER AS PERCENT OF	
		Last Year	Average †
Blue River	7	153	153
Colorado	20	123	138
Plateau	3	55	82
Roaring Fork	7	90	109
Williams Fork	2	110	132
Willow	2	100	132

SOIL MOISTURE

RIVER BASIN	Number of Stations	THIS YEAR'S MOISTURE as PERCENT OF:	
		Last Year	Average †
Blue River	1	115	111
Colorado	4	118	111
Roaring Fork	1	127	125
Willow	1	112	96

RESERVOIR STORAGE (Thousand Ac. Ft.) END OF MONTH

RESERVOIR	Usable Capacity	Usable Storage		
		This Year	Last Year	Average †
Dillon	254	239	237	130
Granby	466	264	147	233
Green Mountain	147	71	83	63
Homestake	43	18	17	---

RESERVOIR STORAGE (Thousand Ac. Ft.) END OF MONTH

RESERVOIR	Usable Capacity	Usable Storage		
		This Year	Last Year	Average †
Ruedi	101	75	---	---
Williams Fork	97	46	25	27
Willow Creek	9	7	7	6
Vega	32	14	11	11

+ 1953-1967 period.

*This year in percent of avg.

Return if not delivered
UNITED STATES DEPARTMENT OF AGRICULTURE
SOIL CONSERVATION SERVICE
SNOW SURVEY
COLORADO STATE UNIVERSITY
FORT COLLINS, COLORADO 80521

OFFICIAL BUSINESS

POSTAGE AND FEES PAID
U S DEPARTMENT OF AGRICULTURE

FIRST CLASS MAIL

CO-7b

WATER SUPPLY OUTLOOK
FOR THE SOIL CONSERVATION DISTRICTS IN THE
YAMPA, WHITE, AND NORTH PLATTE RIVER WATERSHEDS
IN COLORADO
as of
March 1, 1970

U.S. DEPARTMENT OF AGRICULTURE · SOIL CONSERVATION SERVICE
COLORADO EXPERIMENT STATION, STATE ENGINEERS OF COLORADO AND NEW MEXICO

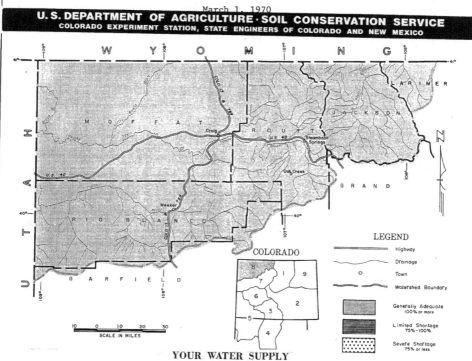

LEGEND

━━━━ Highway
──── Drainage
○ Town
━ ━ Watershed Boundary

Generally Adequate
100% or more

Limited Shortage
75%-100%

Severe Shortage
75% or less

SCALE IN MILES

YOUR WATER SUPPLY

SNOWFALL IN THIS AREA WAS BELOW NORMAL FOR FEBRUARY. THIS COMBINED WITH ABOVE NORMAL TEMPERATURES HAS REDUCED EXPECTED FLOWS. ALL STREAMS ARE STILL EXPECTED TO FLOW ABOVE NORMAL AND PROVIDE ADEQUATE WATER SUPPLIES THIS SUMMER. FLOW ON SMALL STREAMS SHOULD BE GOOD MOST OF THE YEAR.

SOIL MOISTURE IS STILL REPORTED AS GOOD DESPITE THE WARM TEMPERATURES. MOUNTAIN SOILS ARE GENERALLY WET.

This report prepared by
JACK N. WASHICHEK and RONALD E. MORELAND
SOIL CONSERVATION SERVICE, COLORADO STATE UNIVERSITY
FORT COLLINS, COLORADO

Issued by
F. A. MARK---STATE CONSERVATIONIST   R. L. PORTER---AREA CONSERVATIONIST
U. S. DEPARTMENT OF AGRICULTURE - SOIL CONSERVATION SERVICE
DENVER, COLORADO   GLENWOOD SPRINGS, COLORADO

The Conservation of Water begins with the Snow Survey

STREAMFLOW FORECASTS (1000 Ac. Ft.)

FORECAST POINT and Forecast Period	Forecast	Apr-Sept *	Average +
Elk at Clark	200	105	191
Laramie at Jelm	149	143	104
Little Snake at Lily	400	144	277
No. Platte at Northgate			
White nr Meeker	300	102	293
Yampa nr Maybell	900	105	853
Yampa at Steamboat Springs	295	113	260

WATER SUPPLY OUTLOOK

Expressed as "Poor, Fair, Average, Excellent" With Respect to Usual Supply

STREAM or AREA	Flow Period	
	Spring Season	Late Season
Canadian River	Exc.	Avg.
Hunt Creek	Exc.	Avg.
Illinois River	Exc.	Avg.
Michigan River	Exc.	Avg.
Oak Creek	Exc.	Avg.
Trout Creek	Exc.	Avg.

SUMMARY of SNOW MEASUREMENTS
(COMPARISON WITH PREVIOUS YEARS)

RIVER BASIN and/or SUB-WATERSHED	Number of Courses Averaged	THIS YEAR'S SNOW WATER AS PERCENT OF	
		Last Year	Average +
Elk	2	83	93
Laramie	2	124	134
North Platte	5	104	125
White	2	97	107
Yampa	5	105	120

SOIL MOISTURE

RIVER BASIN	Number of Stations	THIS YEAR'S MOISTURE as PERCENT OF:	
		Last Year	Average +
Laramie	2	173	148
North Platte	2	117	105
Yampa	1	70	52

+ 1953-1967 period.

*This year in percent of avg.

Return if not delivered
UNITED STATES DEPARTMENT OF AGRICULTURE
SOIL CONSERVATION SERVICE
SNOW SURVEY
COLORADO STATE UNIVERSITY
FORT COLLINS, COLORADO 80521

OFFICIAL BUSINESS

POSTAGE AND FEES PAID
U S DEPARTMENT OF AGRICULTURE

FIRST CLASS MAIL

CO-8b

WATER SUPPLY OUTLOOK
FOR THE SOIL CONSERVATION DISTRICTS IN THE
LOWER SOUTH PLATTE RIVER WATERSHED IN COLORADO
as of

March 1, 1970

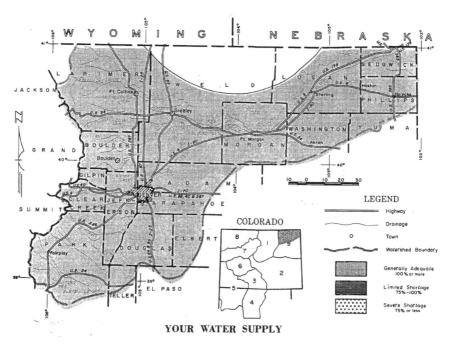

YOUR WATER SUPPLY

THE SNOW PACK ON THE SOUTH PLATTE DRAINAGE CONTINUES TO BE MUCH ABOVE AVERAGE. SUMMER WATER SUPPLIES SHOULD BE ADEQUATE. STREAMFLOW FORECASTS RANGE FROM 116% ON THE CACHE LA POUDRE TO 136% ON THE ST. VRAIN.

RESERVOIR STORAGE IS GOOD WITH 111% OF LAST YEAR AND 125% OF THE 1953-67 AVERAGE.

SOIL MOISTURE CONDITIONS IN THE IRRIGATED AREAS ARE REPORTED TO BE GOOD. FEBRUARY'S WARM TEMPERATURES HAS DRIED OUT THE SURFACE SOILS.

This report prepared by

JACK N. WASHICHEK and RONALD E. MORELAND
SOIL CONSERVATION SERVICE, COLORADO STATE UNIVERSITY
FORT COLLINS, COLORADO

Issued by

F A MARK—STATE CONSERVATIONIST   J.L. HALL—AREA CONSERVATIONIST
U. S. DEPARTMENT OF AGRICULTURE - SOIL CONSERVATION SERVICE
DENVER, COLORADO   STERLING, COLORADO

The Conservation of Water begins with the Snow Survey

STREAMFLOW FORECASTS (1000 Ac. Ft.) Apr–Sept

FORECAST POINT and Forecast Period	Forecast	*	Average †
Big Thompson at Drake (2)	125	125	100
Boulder at Orodell	60	122	49
Cache La Poudre at Canon Mouth (1)	250	116	215
Clear Cr. at Golden (3)	160	134	119
Saint Vrain at Lyons	95	136	70

(1) Observed flow plus by-pass to power plants.
(2) Observed flow minus diversions through August P. Gumlick Tunnel.
(3) Observed flow plus change in storage in Price Reservoir.

WATER SUPPLY OUTLOOK
Expressed as "Poor, Fair, Average, Excellent" With Respect to Usual Supply.

STREAM or AREA	Flow Period	
	Spring Season	Late Season
South Platte from Greeley to Ft. Morgan	Exc.	Avg.
South Platte from Ft. Morgan to Sterling	Exc.	Avg.
South Platte below Sterling	Exc.	Avg.

SUMMARY of SNOW MEASUREMENTS
(COMPARISON WITH PREVIOUS YEARS)

RIVER BASIN and/or SUB-WATERSHED	Number of Courses Averaged	THIS YEAR'S SNOW WATER AS PERCENT OF	
		Last Year	Average †
Big Thompson	5	156	146
Boulder	3	192	140
Cache La Poudre	8	133	145
Clear Creek	6	174	146
Saint Vrain	2	179	149
South Platte	3	163	147

SOIL MOISTURE

RIVER BASIN	Number of Stations	THIS YEAR'S MOISTURE as PERCENT OF:	
		Last Year	Average †
Big Thompson	3	136	124
Boulder	1	87	92
Cache La Poudre	2	173	148
Clear Creek	2	128	110
Saint Vrain	2	119	119
South Platte	2	107	100

RESERVOIR STORAGE (Thousand Ac. Ft.) END OF MONTH

RESERVOIR	Usable Capacity	Usable Storage		
		This Year	Last Year	Average †
Carter	108.9	91.3	90.3	71.3
Cheesman	79.0	79.1	40.6	46.4
Eleven Mile	97.8	96.4	94.6	72.0
Empire	37.7	29.9	31.3	27.2
Horsetooth	143.5	93.3	98.4	93.6

RESERVOIR STORAGE (Thousand Ac. Ft.) END OF MONTH

RESERVOIR	Usable Capacity	Usable Storage		
		This Year	Last Year	Average †
Jackson	35.4	30.5	31.5	30.8
Julesburg	28.2	20.1	20.5	20.7
Prewitt	32.8	25.6	8.8	14.5
Point of Rocks	70.0	66.2	62.2	49.9
Riverside	57.5	53.9	52.9	44.6

+ 1953–1967 period.

Return if not delivered
UNITED STATES DEPARTMENT OF AGRICULTURE
SOIL CONSERVATION SERVICE
SNOW SURVEY
COLORADO STATE UNIVERSITY
FORT COLLINS, COLORADO 80521

OFFICIAL BUSINESS

*This year in percent of avg.

POSTAGE AND FEES PAID
U S DEPARTMENT OF AGRICULTURE

FIRST CLASS MAIL

CO-9b

APPENDIX I

SNOW COURSE MEASUREMENTS as of March 1, 1970

SNOW COURSE	DATE OF SURVEY	SNOW DEPTH (INCHES)	WATER CONTENT (INCHES)	WATER CONTENT (INCHES) LAST YEAR	AVG. 53-67
NORTH PLATTE BASIN					
Laramie River					
Deadman Hill	2/27	57	17.9	15.5	12.6
McIntyre	NS		--	--	--
Roach	2/25	63	18.2	13.5	14.4
North Platte River					
Cameron Pass	2/26	73	27.0	25.1	18.8
Columbine Lodge	2/26	72	23.5	21.3	19.6
Northgate	2/26	26	7.0	7.0	5.3
Park View	2/24	35	9.5	9.5	7.2
Willow Cr. Pass(B)	2/24	42	12.1	13.2	9.8
SOUTH PLATTE BASIN					
Boulder Creek					
Baltimore	2/26	35	8.7	4.3	5.8
Boulder Falls	2/27	47	14.6	8.4	9.1
University Camp	2/27	59	19.5	9.6	15.6
Big Thompson River					
Deer Ridge	2/27	28	8.2	3.1	3.9
Hidden Valley	2/26	42	11.3	7.2	7.9
Lake Irene (B)	2/26	68	22.3	16.4	18.2
Long's Peak	2/28	41	11.3	6.9	8.0
Two Mile	2/26	58	17.3	11.4	10.9
Cache La Poudre					
Bennett Creek	2/27	32	9.9	5.3	--
Big South	3/1	8	2.2	0.4	2.4
Cameron Pass	2/26	73	27.0	25.1	18.8
Chambers Lake	3/1	39	12.3	7.2	7.2
Deadman Hill	2/27	57	17.9	15.5	12.6
Hour Glass Lake	2/27	33	9.4	4.9	5.1
Joe Wright	2/26	72	25.1	19.5	--
Lost Lake	3/1	44	14.2	8.4	9.6
Pine Creek	2/26	4	1.1	1.9	1.6
Red Feather	2/26	25	6.9	5.1	5.6
Clear Creek					
Baltimore (B)	2/26	35	8.7	4.3	5.8
Berthoud Falls	2/26	56	15.6	9.0	11.5
Empire	2/26	32	9.7	4.1	6.0
Grizzly Peak (B)	2/25	70	23.2	13.5	13.4
Loveland Lift	2/26	64	20.6	13.0	17.7
Loveland Pass	2/26	58	19.4	12.0	12.3
Saint Vrain River					
Copeland Lake	2/25	22	5.6	3.5	3.7
Ward	2/26	28	7.1	3.6	4.8
Wild Basin	NS			--	9.7
South Platte River					
Como	2/26	37	9.4	4.4	--
Geneva Park	2/25	30	6.0	2.4	3.1
Horseshoe Mt.	2/25	47	12.4	8.0	--
Hoosier Pass	2/27	51	13.9	9.4	10.5
Jefferson Creek	2/26	43	11.0	7.2	7.4
Mosquito	2/25	48	13.0	7.6	--
Trout Creek Pass	2/25	24	4.9	3.8	--
ARKANSAS BASIN					
Arkansas River					
Bigelow Divide	2/25	28	6.2	2.4	4.8
Cooper Hill (B)	2/27	48	12.8	8.8	8.5
East Fork	2/25	42	11.8	8.3	7.6
Four Mile Park	2/26	26	6.7	4.4	4.6
Fremont Pass	2/26	59	17.0	12.7	12.4
Garfield	2/26	37	11.4	11.6	11.4
Hermit Lake	2/25	20	6.1	--	--
Monarch Pass	2/26	49	15.0	14.5	14.3
Tennessee Pass	2/26	43	10.3	8.2	8.5
Twin Lakes Tunnel	2/28	38	10.9	6.8	8.6
Westcliffe	2/25	22	5.0	6.0	5.7

SNOW COURSE	DATE OF SURVEY	SNOW DEPTH (INCHES)	WATER CONTENT (INCHES)	WATER CONTENT (INCHES) LAST YEAR	AVG. 53-67
Cucharas River					
Blue Lakes	2/26	13	2.6	--	3.5
Cucharas Pass	2/26	27	5.8	3.9	--
LaVeta Pass (B)	2/26	21	5.0	7.0	7.8
Purgatorie River					
Bourbon	2/25	29	5.0	5.1	6.4
RIO GRANDE BASIN—Colo.					
Alamosa River					
Silver Lakes	2/26	7	1.7	7.2	5.5
Summitville (A)	2/28	46	8.2	17.0	14.6
Conejos River					
Cumbres (A)	2/28	22	6.2	24.5	16.5
Platoro (A)	2/28	32	9.4	15.5	13.8
River Springs	2/27	7	1.8	7.4	5.8
Culebra River					
Brown Cabin	2/28	9	3.1	4.8	--
Cottonwood (B)	NS			6.5	--
Culebra	2/26	25	5.6	7.9	7.3
LaVeta Pass (B)	2/26	21	5.0	7.0	7.8
Trinchera (B)	2/28	24	5.4	6.2	--
Rio Grande					
Cochetopa Pass	2/25	36	8.4	3.4	4.5
Grayback	NS			--	--
Hiway	2/26	45	13.3	25.2	21.4
Lake Humphrey	2/27	13	2.9	5.4	6.2
Love Lake (A)	2/28	16	4.0	5.4	--
Pass Creek	2/26	14	4.2	13.2	10.8
Pool Table	2/27	18	4.2	4.6	5.9
Porcupine	2/27	31	7.4	8.4	8.7
Santa Maria	2/26	5	1.3	5.1	4.4
Upper Rio Grande	3/1	17	2.8	11.0	6.6
Wolf Creek Pass	2/26	47	13.0	29.3	22.9
Wolf Cr. Sum. (B)	2/26	56	17.5	28.0	22.1
RIO GRANDE BASIN—N.M.					
Pecos River					
Panchuela	2/24	1	0.2	3.3	3.2
Rio Chama					
Bateman	2/26	26	6.2	13.9	9.4
Capulin Peak	2/26	9	2.7	6.6	4.5
Chama Divide	2/27	0	0.0	6.7	3.6
Chamita	2/27	14	3.3	13.3	7.9
Rio Grande					
Aspen Grove	2/26	9	2.8	4.3	5.2
Big Tesuque	2/25	3	1.0	6.8	4.6
Bluebird Mesa	2/25	5	1.3	6.2	4.7
Cordova (A)	2/28	21	6.5	10.8	9.7
Elk Cabin	2/26	4	1.0	1.7	3.3
Fenton Hill	2/26	2	0.4	6.2	3.9
Pajarito Peak	2/26	0	0.0	1.0	1.5
Payrole (A)	2/28	19	4.0	9.8	7.8
Quemazon	2/26	21	4.5	7.6	7.7
Rio En Medio	2/25	15	5.1	10.0	7.9
Sandoval	2/25	6	1.4	4.7	5.0
Taos Canyon	2/26	7	1.6	5.9	4.4
Tres Ritos	2/26	10	3.6	5.3	4.8
Rio Hondo					
Twinning	2/26	21	6.1	9.9	--
Red River					
Hematite Park (B)	2/25	6	1.5	3.3	3.7
Red River	2/25	16	3.4	5.7	5.2

NOTE: NS - No Survey
(A) - Air Observed
(B) - On Adjacent Drainage

SNOW COURSE MEASUREMENTS as of March 1, 1970

SNOW COURSE	CURRENT INFORMATION DATE OF SURVEY	SNOW DEPTH (INCHES)	WATER CONTENT (INCHES)	PAST RECORD WATER CONTENT (INCHES) LAST YEAR	AVG 53 67
SAN JUAN-DOLORES BASIN					
Animas River					
Cascade	2/26	14	3.7	18.4	10.2
Lemon	2/25	0	0.0	14.7	- -
Mineral Creek	2/26	40	11.4	17.9	11.7
Molas Lake	2/26	30	8.2	15.6	11.0
Purgatory	2/26	46	12.3	22.4	- -
Red Mt. Pass (B)	2/26	74	24.1	30.3	23.5
Silverton Sub-Sta.	2/26	10	2.6	11.1	5.6
Spud Mountain	2/26	41	12.3	28.6	19.5
Dolores River					
Lizzard Head	2/26	42	12.0	20.1	12.6
Lone Cone	2/27	38	11.2	19.7	- -
Rico	2/26	12	4.1	14.9	6.8
Telluride	2/26	31	8.2	9.0	5.9
Trout Lake	2/26	35	10.9	16.0	10.7
San Juan River					
Chama Divide (B)	2/27	0	0.0	6.7	3.6
Chamita (B)	2/27	14	3.3	13.3	7.9
Upper San Juan	2/26	45	12.9	34.6	25.2
Wolf Cr. Pass (B)	2/26	47	13.0	29.3	22.9
Wolf C. Summit	2/26	56	17.5	28.0	22.1
GUNNISON BASIN					
Gunnison River					
Alexander Lake	2/25	52	16.9	25.0	17.0
Blue Mesa	2/24	30	7.6	9.6	3.5
Butte	2/27	46	13.3	15.6	- -
Cochetopa Pass (B)	2/25	36	8.4	3.4	4.5
Crested Butte	2/26	37	11.1	15.6	10.6
Keystone	2/26	57	17.9	21.1	16.3
Lake City	2/24	33	7.6	6.0	7.6
Mesa Lakes (B)	2/26	42	12.7	19.7	13.4
McClure Pass	2/27	37	13.0	16.5	14.6
Park Cone	2/26	36	12.3	11.6	8.8
Park Reservoir	2/26	55	15.2	31.1	19.6
Porphyry Creek	2/26	49	15.4	13.7	13.9
Tomichi	2/26	37	11.7	11.1	10.2
Surface Creek					
Alexander Lake	2/25	52	16.9	25.0	17.0
Mesa Lakes (B)	2/26	42	12.7	19.7	13.4
Park Reservoir	2/26	54	15.2	31.1	19.6
Uncompahgre River					
Ironton Park	2/24	41	13.1	14.3	10.4
Red Mountain Pass	2/26	74	24.1	30.3	23.5
Telluride (B)	2/26	31	8.2	9.0	5.9
COLORADO BASIN					
Blue River					
Blue River	2/27	40	10.9	6.4	7.3
Fremont Pass	2/26	59	17.0	12.7	12.4
Frisco	2/25	36	10.4	6.5	6.3
Grizzly Peak	2/25	70	23.2	13.5	13.4
Hoosier Pass (B)	2/25	51	13.9	9.4	10.5
Shrine Pass	2/25	67	21.4	14.3	13.6
Snake River	2/25	38	10.9	7.5	6.7
Summit Ranch	2/25	29	7.7	- -	6.0

SNOW COURSE	CURRENT INFORMATION DATE OF SURVEY	SNOW DEPTH (INCHES)	WATER CONTENT (INCHES)	PAST RECORD WATER CONTENT (INCHES) LAST YEAR	AVG 53 67
Colorado River					
Arrow	2/27	44	15.3	10.9	9.3
Berthoud Pass	2/26	56	16.1	12.1	11.6
Berthoud Summit	2/26	68	19.0	11.9	14.8
Cooper Hill	2/27	48	12.8	8.8	8.5
Fiddler Gulch	NS			- -	13.5
Glenmar Ranch	2/24	32	8.4	8.0	6.4
Gore Pass	2/25	35	10.5	9.9	8.4
Grand Lake	2/25	32	8.2	8.5	6.6
Lake Irene	2/26	68	22.3	16.4	18.2
Lapland	3/2	40	12.1	9.8	8.6
Lulu	2/26	67	22.0	14.7	13.2
Lynx Pass	2/25	43	12.2	12.2	10.0
McKenzie Gulch	2/27	22	4.9	8.0	4.8
Middle Fork	2/24	36	10.0	8.8	7.5
Milner	2/26	48	15.0	13.2	11.1
North Inlet	2/25	33	9.1	9.0	7.4
Pando	2/25	41	12.4	10.5	7.9
Phantom Valley	2/26	41	12.1	11.4	8.5
Ranch Creek	2/27	39	11.5	8.5	7.1
Tennessee Pass(B)	2/26	43	10.3	8.2	8.5
Vail Pass	2/25	63	20.6	15.1	14.0
Vasquez	2/25	51	13.9	9.8	9.5
Roaring Fork River					
Aspen	2/25	52	13.8	16.4	13.0
Chapman	2/25	53	15.9	12.9	- -
Independence Pass	2/28	55	15.4	14.2	13.9
Ivanhoe	2/25	62	19.5	15.2	13.8
Kiln	2/24	44	11.8	11.2	- -
Last Chance	2/24	32	9.8	9.2	- -
Lift	2/25	53	15.2	17.0	13.8
McClure Pass	2/27	37	13.0	16.5	14.6
Nast	2/24	26	6.5	7.9	5.2
North Lost Trail	2/27	39	12.1	18.8	13.0
Williams Fork River					
Glenmar Ranch	2/24	32	8.4	8.0	6.4
Jones Pass	2/26	57	17.3	12.2	10.9
Middle Fork	2/24	36	10.0	8.8	7.5
Willow Creek					
Granby	2/24	30	8.9	7.8	6.1
Willow Cr. Pass	2/24	42	12.1	13.2	9.8
Plateau Creek					
Mesa Lakes	2/26	42	12.7	19.7	13.4
Park Reservoir	2/26	54	15.2	31.1	19.6
Trickle Divide	2/26	56	16.7	30.9	21.1
YAMPA BASIN					
Elk River					
Clark	2/27	33	8.9	13.4	11.5
Elk River	2/27	51	16.2	16.9	15.5
Hahn's Peak	2/27	41	12.2	15.3	- -
White River					
Burro Mountain	2/26	48	15.3	16.1	15.2
Rio Blanco	2/27	38	14.9	15.2	12.9
Yampa River					
Bear River	NS			- -	- -
Columbine Lodge(B)	2/26	72	23.5	21.3	19.6
Dry Lake	2/25	56	18.8	19.2	17.6
Lynx Pass (B)	2/25	43	12.2	12.2	10.0
Rabbit Ears	2/26	77	27.0	24.4	21.2
Yampa View	2/26	47	15.5	15.3	12.3

NS – No Survey
(B) – On Adjacent Drainage

APPENDIX II

STATION	DATE OF SURVEY	CAPACITY (INCHES)	THIS YEAR	LAST YEAR	AVG. ALL DATA
NORTH PLATTE BASIN					
North Platte River					
Muddy Pass	11/13/69	11.1	7.4	6.1	6.4
Willow Pass	11/14/69	9.5	6.4	5.7	6.7
SOUTH PLATTE BASIN					
Boulder Creek					
Alpine Camp	11/14/69	6.9	3.4	3.9	3.7
Big Thompson River					
Beaver Dam	10/23/69	7.1	5.5	3.6	3.8
Guard Station	10/23/69	6.9	3.4	2.9	3.4
Two Mile	10/23/69	9.1	6.9	5.1	5.5
Clear Creek					
Clear Creek	11/19/69	9.5	7.7	5.7	7.1
Hoop Creek	11/19/69	4.9	3.3	2.9	2.9
Cache La Poudre River					
Feather	11/4/69	10.1	8.3	4.0	4.5
Laramie Road	11/4/69	12.4	9.9	6.5	7.8
South Platte River					
Hoosier Pass	11/13/69	7.8	4.8	4.7	4.9
Kenosha Pass	11/13/69	4.4	2.7	2.3	2.6
ARKANSAS BASIN					
Arkansas River					
Garfield	10/30/69	6.7	4.4	3.1	3.9
Leadville	11/19/69	7.8	4.8	4.0	4.2
Twin Lakes Tunnel	11/13/69	4.5	1.6	0.9	2.3
RIO GRANDE BASIN - COLORADO					
Conejos River					
Mogote	10/31/69	10.7	7.1	4.7	5.5
Rio Grande					
Alberta Park	10/30/69	8.2	5.8	4.9	5.0
Bristol View	10/30/69	6.1	5.9	2.9	3.9
LaVeta	10/31/69	11.9	8.2	10.0	7.2
RIO GRANDE BASIN - NEW MEXICO					
Rio Chama					
Bateman	2/26/70	6.7	1.3	1.3	3.2
Chamita	2/27/70	8.0	4.0	5.0	4.1
Rio Grande					
Aqua Piedra	2/27/70	7.2	4.4	4.2	3.7
Big Tesuque	2/25/70	3.7	0.9	2.0	1.9
Fenton Hill	11/25/69	6.5	5.7	2.1	3.8
Rio En Medio	2/25/70	3.5	0.4	0.4	1.2
Taos Canyon	2/26/70	3.3	1.6	4.2	2.3
Red River					
Red Summit	2/25/70	4.8	1.5	1.6	1.9
ANIMAS - SAN JUAN BASINS					
Animas River					
Cascade	11/12/69	9.1	5.9	3.3	6.3
Mineral Creek	11/12/69	5.7	2.6	2.1	3.7
Molas Lake	11/12/69	9.4	4.5	3.0	4.6
Dolores River					
Dolores	11/12/69	19.6	8.2	9.8	6.7
Lizzard Head	11/12/69	11.8	4.4	3.7	8.3
Rico	11/12/69	13.8	10.4	5.5	9.9

APPENDIX II

SOIL MOISTURE MEASUREMENTS as of March 1, 1970

STATION	DATE OF SURVEY	CAPACITY (INCHES)	THIS YEAR	LAST YEAR	AVG. ALL DATA
GUNNISON BASIN					
Gunnison River					
King	10/30/69	3.3	2.2	2.1	1.9
COLORADO BASIN (Mainstem)					
Blue River					
Blue River	11/13/69	4.2	3.1	2.7	2.8
Colorado River					
Berthoud Pass	10/15/69	3.9	3.2	1.9	2.8
Gore	11/16/69	4.9	3.3	- -	2.5
Grand Mesa	10/15/69	12.5	9.3	8.5	9.3
Ranch Creek	10/15/69	8.7	5.7	5.0	6.0
Vail	11/19/69	12.3	9.5	8.1	6.9
Roaring Fork River					
Placita	12/2/69	9.3	6.5	5.1	5.2
YAMPA BASIN					
Yampa River					
Hahn's Peak	12/4/69	19.0	6.1	8.7	11.8

LIST of COOPERATORS

The following organizations cooperate in snow surveys for the Colorado, Platte, Arkansas and Rio Grande watersheds. Many other organizations and individuals furnish valuable information for the snow survey reports. Their cooperation is gratefully acknowledged.

STATE

Colorado State Engineer
New Mexico State Engineer
Nebraska State Engineer
Colorado Experiment Station
Rocky Mountain Forest and Range Experiment Station

FEDERAL

Department of Agriculture

Forest Service
Soil Conservation Service

Department of Interior

Bureau of Reclamation
Geological Survey
National Park Service
Indian Service

Department of Commerce

Weather Bureau

War Department

Army Engineer Corps

Atomic Energy Commission

INVESTOR OWNED UTILITIES

Colorado Public Service Company
Public Service Company of New Mexico

MUNICIPALITIES

City of Denver   City of Greeley
City of Boulder   City of Fort Collins

WATER USERS ORGANIZATIONS

Arkansas Valley Ditch Association
Colorado River Water Conservation District

IRRIGATION PROJECTS

Farmers Reservoir and Irrigation Company
San Luis Valley Irrigation District
Santa Maria Reservoir Company
Costilla Land Company
Uncompahgre Valley Water Users' Association
Twin Lakes Reservoir and Canal Company
Trinchera Irrigation Co.

CPSIA information can be obtained
at www.ICGtesting.com
Printed in the USA
BVHW041132180119
538187BV00016B/1148/P